In Defense of the

Riya Aarini

ISBN: 978-1-956496-21-5 (Paperback)

ISBN: 978-1-956496-22-2 (eBook)

Library of Congress Control Number: 2022912732

First published in Austin, Texas, USA

Visit www.riyapresents.com

To those who remember

life has only one guarantee—and it isn't taxes

CONTENTS

CONTENTS

ON REPUTATION

I realize I've got a menacing appearance and a terrible reputation. But personality-wise, I'm not so bad. My looks and bad boy status are all in the name of this unglamorous profession I find myself qualified for. I've got to look and act the part to perform the job convincingly. But don't be fooled by my tattered black robe, the threatening scythe in my hand, and the hollow look I'm famous for. I'm not sure how that hideous representation of me got out in the first place. It's a defamation suit waiting to happen. Unfortunately, the frightening image that I've been associated with since time immemorial appears to be irreversible—and so

1

seems my heartless reputation. It's hard to change the first impressions that shape my hypothetical character. So I'm stuck with this ominous look and scary repute forever. Sure, you'll look twice, and you'll definitely know it's me. But in reality, I'm a super nice guy. Believe me when I say looks are deceiving. When we meet, you'll get to see the nicer side of me. I promise.

ON BAD TIMING

Look, I know you've got big plans ahead, and I may arrive at an inopportune time. But I've got big plans too—basically, I've got a job to do. I'm on a schedule here, and I need to stick to it. Timewise, my meeting with you may be a tad inconvenient. When I show up, you might be lying on the hospital operating table undergoing cardiac bypass surgery, or have just received that awesome promotion you've been working hard to earn for the past three years, or be shocked with surprise by an overenthusiastic crowd at your fifty-sixth birthday celebration. I completely understand your predicament. But hear me out. Our schedules are

3

bound to conflict. Sadly, almost no one is ever ready for me. So bear with me when we meet, and try holding off your relentless complaints about my notoriously bad timing.

ON DEATH AND TAXES

I know I'm unavoidable, but you're putting me right up there with taxes? Come on! You can do better than that. I'm actually aghast to be likened to one of the greatest ills in the universe. I, for one, am not as bad as taxes. I mean, I don't follow you around year after year pilfering from your shallow pockets. I come around once in a lifetime. And that's it! Taxes, though, take a less noble path and haunt you night and day. You can always expect taxes around the bend. You know they're coming soon enough. There's no way around . . . taxes. It's hard even for someone as worldly wise as me to get the word out of my mouth; I practically puke when I say it. Listen, no one is immune from paying taxes in this universe, not even me. And to think I'd get a tax break because I deliver souls. Hmph. Not so.

ON THINKING OF ME

I never get a card in the mail. No one picks up the phone to say hello. Have you ever sent me a nice email? For heaven's sake, it gets lonely doing my solo job night and day. Isolation is never a healthy thing. A little caring gesture, a friendly smile, or a welcoming wave from across the park would be nice. Is it so terrible to be pleasant to a grim reaper? I mean, there aren't too many people out there for me to get close to. I can be flexible with who's in my social circle—if anyone wanted to be included in mine, that is. But no one does, and I've got social needs too. Seriously, not a soul thinks of me until I'm knocking on their door and ready to whisk them away.

7

ON HAVING SUPERFANS

Most of my appointments flee when I approach. And that's all fine and dandy, because my work is over in a jiffy. I'm not seeking a long-term relationship. I'm just here to do my job. Plus, given my workload, I don't have time to chitchat with my appointments before I whisk them away to their forever afterlife. I'm not going to stand by and discuss the unbearably humid weather or the strikeouts in baseball or my favorite ethnic cuisine. It's not in the job description, so I'm not going to bother. But a special few have a morbid fascination for me and actually seek me out just for the thrill. It's these folks from whom *I* tend to flee. It's always tricky when they're next on my list, because I have to be extremely careful. If I'm not, they'll cling to me and never let go. It'll be me leading an innocent soul to an afterlife while the morbid superfan clutches the edges of my robe like a fanged bat clutching its prey. It's not an ideal situation and makes me appear a tad unprofessional. I swear, having stalker fans is never a blessing in disguise.

ON HAVING A THANKLESS JOB

I never receive praise for performing the invaluable work I do, not a single "You didn't make a mess, Reaper" or "That was fast, dude" or "Painless, thanks." Instead, everyone runs away from me in the opposite direction screaming and yelling at the top of their lungs and flailing their arms wildly. Sometimes, I look in the mirror and, with a sniffle, ask myself, "Am I really that frightening?" Then I comfort myself with, "Nah, I've got mysterious allure." All the resistance makes my job all the more difficult. Without me, the planet would be overpopulated, and the quality of life would be horribly poor. A small thank-you after delivering every few million souls would be appreciated. I make room for all the adorable new life, after all. Have some gratitude for my services, please.

ON HOW WE MEET

I'm number two here, taking orders from the big guy upstairs. So when you're scheduled to be next, come peaceably. I realize you have no control over how we'll meet, and it can provoke an extreme case of anxiety when I'm close. I mean, it's understandable to feel angst if you've lived a somewhat corrupt life and are expecting an uncomfortable afterlife. Even those who've lived an admirably moral life might feel the jitters not knowing for certain whether they will be delivered to the Elysian Fields. No one's perfect, not even me. But worry not. The man upstairs has it all figured out. I'm just the delivery guy, ready to carry your soul to the place it most deserves.

ON VICTIMHOOD

It bothers me terribly when my next appointment is referred to as my next victim. I don't know how that dreadfully wrong term got around. My appointments are never my victims, not in any sense of the word. I perform an invaluable service to my *clients*. How else do you think your soul is delivered safely to the otherworldly realm? Sure, it's only a one-time meet-and-greet-type thing and off we go, but my work is important in continuing the circle of life. Plus, I consider my clients to be equally precious, since they keep me working and on the payroll. Without them, I'd be in dire straits. So consider yourself a priceless client—not an intended victim. Please, be classy.

ON CHEATING ME

I know you want to escape me, and you'll do anything to achieve that end. Try as you might, you can't cheat the grim reaper. Let me tell you a thing or two. I've had appointments who have faked their own deaths, disappearing to distant tropical islands on speedboats loaded with all the liquor, jewelry, and SPF 15 sunscreen that money can buy. Everyone believed they checked out, even holding the loveliest of funerals, with flowers and hundreds of guests, the whole shebang. I may look like a tool, but, mind you, I'm no fool. I've found every appointment on my schedule, no matter where in the farthest corners of the earth they hid. It unnerves me that you'd think I'm stupid enough to fall for your schemes. I mean, I've been around the block gazillions of times, and I've seen it all through the ages. I know every trick in the book. In fact, for kicks, I published a book of ruses that my appointments have attempted; it's called *1,001 Ways to Escape the Grim Reaper*—and it sold pretty darn well! I hope it doesn't give my future appointments any ideas. It'll make finding them all the more time consuming.

ON NEEDING THERAPY

I admit I'm not as emotionally strong as I seem. I come across as fierce and confident—but that's part of the persona expected from my profession. See, I've got a job that no one else in the universe wants. Can you blame me for being crabby? I'm stuck in this job, and it's sometimes hard to handle. The nature of my work is unlike any other, and there's not too many like-minded professionals out there who can understand the complexities involved in what I do. Being a grim reaper who manages the itineraries of countless souls is never a simple task. Venting to a support group is also impossible, because no one can relate to the particulars of my job. I'd be the odd one out in the group—and that makes me squeamish. To cope with all my work-related troubles, I immerse myself in therapy once a week, you know, just to keep all the nuts and bolts in good working order. I wouldn't want to go bananas. It'd be bad for business.

ON WORKING MYSELF TO THE BONE

Yꞌou've got to have sympathy for someone in my position. All I do is work night and day. I meet with appointments every second. I know I get to travel the world for my job, but I've circled the earth centillions and centillions of times, and it gets a little tedious. I've seen it all. After all, I've been doing this job since time immemorial. Sure, the species change over the millennia, but the nature of the job doesn't. Breaks are unheard of in my profession. You know, every now and then I feel like a well-oiled machine working at full speed in a factory day in and day out. The pay is nothing to brag about either. I can't even afford a new robe, like one without the frayed edges that give me the pathetic look of a lost soul. Wouldn't it be special if I got a break, maybe for a few months or a year, so I could travel for leisure rather than work? It'd be fabulous if I got a breather—and it'd probably be appreciated by all.

ON MY PEARLY WHITES

Have you ever seen me with a bad set of teeth? I think not! Every image of me shows off my fabulous, perfectly straight pearly whites. I enjoy highly skilled dental care, courtesy of my great dental insurance, which gives me access to some of the bravest dentists around. I've never had a root canal go wrong. My ivories are perfectly aligned, flawlessly white, and firmly in place. You won't see me with serious tooth loss and a subsequent full set of dentures, because I'm proud to say I've kept up on my oral hygiene and have all my original teeth—yep, even after all the wear and tear over eternity. But imagine that, a grim reaper with dentures.

With my luck, my dentures would humiliatingly pop out at the most inconvenient time, like when I laugh hideously at our first and only meeting. You'd be shocked to death, and so would I.

ON THE DANCE OF DEATH

Let's make one thing clear: I don't spin, step, or get down. I don't live for the tango or the freestyle or the waltz. You'll never see me line dancing or pretending that I know what I'm doing under the strobe lights glittering on the dance floor. You'll never catch me in a sparkly sequined outfit and heels designed to express my rebellious side. My job is to transport your soul, not tempt you into the afterworld with a dance. Maybe you'll stumble upon an eager dancer at the trendy disco club on the corner of Fifth Avenue and Park. I'm flattered, really, that you think of me when you slip on your dancing shoes and paint the town red.

Whether you wildly swing your hips past midnight with an attractive royal, a dirty-faced peddler, or someone equal to your social status, I'm never far. I've got a glitzy reputation as the great equalizer; still, dancing is not my thing. So find yourself a willing partner, because the grim reaper doesn't dance.

ON BEING MYSTERIOUS

I'm known the world over for having a mysterious air about me. The afterlife, after all, is unknown. Who better to transport your soul to the other world than someone as mysterious as me? It's understandable to feel frightened when you don't have a clue as to where I'm about to take you. I guess that's why it works so well that grim is my name and fright is my game. As I'm an enigmatic, shadowy figure, you'll never figure me out. You'll also never know when I'm about to make my appearance. The uncertainty around our meeting makes my job all the more fun. It's the only thing that keeps me going. If my whole persona weren't shrouded in mystery, I'd be too bored to continue. The promising thing is that you'll never unravel what the afterlife is all about until you're actually there. So keep being uncertain, and I'll keep being mysterious. It's a tried-and-true method.

ON MY SCYTHE

Okay, look, this scythe thing is a little old fashioned. I mean, I don't even think farmers harvest grain with this tool anymore. Harvesting crops nowadays is done by the colossal arms of advanced robotic machines. So why do I still have to wield this ancient relic of the past? I, of all beings, never got the critical update. Again, it just goes to show how much you think of me. Disappointments aside, incorporating today's technology is essential for someone in my eternal position. I'm an early adopter of the latest and greatest gear. Perhaps a pair of soul-stripping goggles would make my job easier: I simply stare down my appointments as the penetrating red beams of light shoot out from the goggles, and their souls are immediately transported to their respective afterlife. Eh, the glories of automation. Just the thought makes my bones shiver with excitement. Spread the technology around, would you—especially to a grim reaper who's late to the party. Is that too much to ask?

ON GIVING DEATH A FACE

I understand death is entirely abstract, nothing you'd really be able to grasp until that last moment when you make the ultimate exit. But did you really have to choose a skeleton for my face? I mean, really? Of all the things to represent death, you pick something totally unapproachable. Who's going to welcome me when I look like this? You could have done a better job and characterized me as a thing of beauty or wholesomeness or peace, like that mourning dove cooing in the distance. Collecting unwilling souls would be much easier had I been given the innocent face of a gentle bird that is known and loved by all. *Sniffle*. The things you do to make my job difficult.

28

ON MY WORK UNIFORM

I've got a major gripe about my work uniform. It's a tad depressing wearing black head to toe for all of eternity, and it's getting rather painfully dull. The lack of expression is demoralizing too. I mean, it gives the wrong impression that I have no sense of style. As a grim reaper, I've got flair—but my stark wardrobe doesn't reflect it. I'm peeved on all levels. Plus, blending in with the dark matter of outer space, I never stand out, not while wearing what looks like a garbage bag that's been sitting under the sun in the dump for a little too long and failing to decompose. I'd prefer an optimistic color. A bright yellow or a pastel orange, like a delicate sorbet, would have suited me just fine. Yellows would lend some cheer during our appointment. Blues would exude my cool. Pinks would invoke kindness and femininity, just what we all need. But no! Reapers don't get yellows, or blues, or pinks. I'm downright embittered that I'm required to wear solid black until the end of time. I don't even get fun patterns, like polka dots, zigzags, or stripes, which would've been a welcomed embellishment. I wouldn't have even minded plaid. Black does offer some finer attributes, to be fair: it is a color of sophistication. But nothing about what I do is remotely sophisticated. I'm a grim reaper, after all, and sure as day, no one's impressed when they see me. Geez, the things we put up with for a payday.

ON BEING PROMPT

Most of the time, it'll be a surprise when I show up. Okay, so I'm not going to jump out of that three-foot-high cake at your forty-sixth birthday party and yell, "Surprise! Let's go!"—unless I'm scheduled to pick you up precisely at that precious picture-perfect moment. On occasion, you may be told I'm on the way, like after you've received a terminal diagnosis at the medical oncologist's office or escaped from a botched dental surgery or admitted yourself into hospice. I take my job seriously, so you can expect me to be on time, whether that's precisely at 4:06 p.m. or at 2:44 a.m. I work around the clock, and I've gotten used to the pressures over the millennia. On the other hand, I've received last-minute appointments that I learn about just a minute or two before. I've got to hurry my pace to grab the souls as quickly as I can and send them off pronto. Like I said, I'm a professional, and I never miss an appointment. If I did, it'd be a big deal. But have no worries—I've never missed one yet. Have you ever seen a three-thousand-year-old hobbling the streets?

ON APPOINTMENTS

It's funny the way scheduling works. Along with the guy upstairs, I'm the only other being who knows about your appointment with me. You certainly won't until the end is near or upon you. See, some of my appointments are scheduled far in advance. Others, not quite so much. It's always shocking to see that look of surprise when I arrive to pick up someone who's not expecting me. So more often than not, I'm wearing that shocked look too. I feel like it's getting to be a permanent look for me. You even see it in all my pictures, you know, the ones with my dropped jaw—that's my shocked look, if you couldn't tell.

ON PROFESSIONAL EQUIPMENT

Someone screwed up big-time. If I'm supposed to ferry souls to the afterlife, I'll need a boat. And if the boat is going to move forward with you and me in it, I'll need a long oar—or better yet, the latest form of propulsion: a propeller fixed to the back end of the boat. But you never see images of me with the right apparatus for what I consider to be a highly skilled profession: a boat with a propeller and maybe a gargoyle figurehead for the sake of drama. I'm an expert and in high demand. So I need the right gear to perform my job successfully. All you ever see is me carrying a scythe—and I can't maneuver a boat to the other side with a scythe.

It's just impractical. The blade of my scythe would rust upon being exposed to water with every soul I deliver. Plus, it'd take forever to get there, thereby eating away at your precious time in the afterlife. So get with the program, please, and update my image to include a fancy boat meant for two, preferably with an attached propeller. Promoting those old pictures of me wielding a scythe is just misleading the new generations.

ON BEING GRIM

You know, as the personification of death, I've been made to appear rather grim, hence my unpleasant name. But personally, I'm not at all grim, at least when I'm not on the job. I've got a life. Though it's infrequent, when I'm not busy, I enjoy the latest gossip, a delicious craft beer, and a leisurely stroll down the beach on a summer day with a vintage lace parasol in hand. I'm not always hunting souls to deliver to the other worlds. I like having a good time too. But you've unfairly depicted me as grim. In fact, had you painted me with rosy cheeks, a smile on my face, and a full head of hair, passing to the other world would seem so much more agreeable. Would you resist me if I approached you looking beautiful? Instead, I've got this bag of bones for a body and a tattered robe that disgracefully opens up whenever the wind blows, and I wield a pointy scythe. How much grimmer can you get?

ON THE HOURGLASS

Time's up! That's all it means. Why the hourglass?
It's simply the device I've used since the beginning
of the universe to tell me when a soul's time has come.
I rely on the hourglass for scheduling purposes. It's
just the way I've always done things. I could upgrade
to the latest futuristic watch, featuring a world map on
a lacquered dial and telling me the world time across
all twenty-four time zones, so I can see exactly when
and where I need to pick up my next appointment. It'd
make my job far easier and a lot more stylish to have an
automatic, monochromatic gadget. I've been banging
on the door of the man upstairs for years, begging for

an upgrade. But budgets are tight, and my pleas keep falling on deaf ears. So until I get more advanced tools of the trade, I'll just bottle up my frustrations and continue using the old-fashioned—but flawless—hourglass. You have to admit, it does lend a sense of nostalgia to the whole death thing, doesn't it?

ON THE AFTERLIFE

I get it. You dread the moment that last grain of sand falls through the center hole of the hourglass. It's time, and I'm waiting. I'm shaking my head, because most of the time, you don't have to dread. The mysteries of the next world can be, well, mysterious. But remember, the hourglass will be flipped once I pick you up and send you off to your next destination. The whole process begins again, with the newly flipped hourglass ticking off the time you have there. I mean, how many times do you enter a new afterlife? Beats me. I just handle the deliveries. But I'm here to tell you that it's darn well possible that your soul might linger in the afterlife for only a short time, like a couple of hundred years, before it's time to go off to the next world, and the one after that, and so on. No one knows what goes on up there. While I deliver souls to the afterlife's front doorstep, I've never actually been inside.

ON BRIBING ME

I get that you want to try to buy yourself more time, maybe a few months or a couple of years to finish that amazing project and leave your legacy. But a schedule's a schedule. It's final. There's no way around it. You might have gotten it into your head that you can pay off a grim reaper like me. You can't. So don't try. What are you going to do, bribe me with your luxury car? I'm not going to look any classier driving to my next appointment in your sophisticated ride with premium upholstery and the LED mood lighting going—despite a high-performance vehicle being the pinnacle of achievement. Or maybe you think I'll give you three extra months with a studded gold chain across my collarbone and your ex's diamond ring on my bony index finger. Think again, because bribing me with fabulous bling, which has limited worth to a minimalist grim reaper, isn't going to convince me to alter your schedule. Then you get the idea you can tempt me with your five-bedroom house with a hot tub built on the deck. Hmph. There's only so much pleasure a bag of bones can get from soaking in a hot tub, even though I could benefit from a couple of hours' worth of hydrotherapy. But still, with my busy schedule, it's not going to make the cut. So stop wasting your time. Even though I sometimes catch myself considering an attractive deal, you'll never succeed in bribing the grim reaper for a new lease on life.

ON DENYING ME

You can't deny me. I'm as real as the monsoon rains in Phoenix, Arizona. You think you'll live forever, that I'll never come for you, that you'll outwit me. That's all pickled baloney (just ask the pig). I may be a mysterious hooded stranger, and you may only be familiar with my reputation. But there's more to me than repute. Underneath this collection of bones, there's heart and soul. Tenderness aside, since we've never formally met, it's impossible for you to truly know me as an individual. Have you ever had a thoughtful conversation with me? Have you ever dug deep into my soul to find out what drives me? Do you even know what my favorite color is? You'll never enter the depths of who I am until we finally meet and you get a taste of my character as I transport your soul. Just because we haven't met yet, it doesn't mean I don't exist. Just because you've never been face to face with a pangolin or Bigfoot or a spoon-billed sandpiper, it doesn't mean they don't exist. So don't try to deny me. I'm the real deal.

ON BEING OVERWORKED

I'm surprised that I'm not burned out after performing my job impeccably since time began. I mean, I don't even get an assistant. I can imagine it now: Assistants I and II to the Grim Reaper. It's not like I can order Assistant I to pick up a soul at 5:48 p.m. today and command Assistant II to deliver another to the great beyond tomorrow. That's just not how it works. Although, given the demands of my services, I'm open to the prospect of having an assistant or two or two thousand. It'd make my job go all the quicker, and maybe I'd be served a decent cup of espresso every now and then. Making matters worse, this is a one-man job. I handle everything from the initial paperwork to scheduling my arrival and finally delivering your soul. With a little support, I'd actually have some me time, you know, time to spend at the spa or go to the theater for an immersive, out-of-this-world movie experience—which I haven't done in ages. I don't think you'll ever be at the movies digging your fingers into a bucket of artificially flavored butter popcorn, then turning your head to see me seated next to you catching the same movie. It'd be a shock for us both. Given the hectic nature of my job, it'll never happen. Movies and me time are just an overworked grim reaper's dream.

ON COMING AROUND ONCE

I pride myself on not being a pest. I don't go out of my way to annoy a soul. You'll never find me taunting my next appointment with constant updates: "I'm on my way"; "I'll be there in the nick of time"; "I'll see you in five." As a busy grim reaper with a demanding schedule, I don't have the luxury of time to send out updates to every soul I'm about to pick up. It's not discourteous; it's just not in the job description. Instead, I come around just once in a lifetime, unexpectedly most often. That makes me rare, like a shooting star or a blue moon or a clean joke at the comedy club. That's right; I'm rare and therefore priceless. One meeting with me will forever change your life.

ON TRULY LIVING

Listen, a meeting with me has to be earned. If you've lived life well, then you'll have no problem with me once I arrive. A full life is a remarkable one, and you deserve a rest. That's when I come in. I appear at the culmination of a good life. I'm the final curtain to a marvelous play. I'm the starry night to a breathtaking day. I'm the haunting finale to a tear-jerking opera. I'm the ultimate zenith to a soul-wrenching climb to the top of the mountain. There's no avoiding me. It's just a matter of timing—in other words, the exact moment you're scheduled. Have you done enough good deeds to make them smile? Have you laughed yourself silly?

Have you gazed into the sky wondering what else is out there? If you can say yes to the grim reaper's criteria for making it all worthwhile, give yourself a pat on the back; because by the time I arrive, you know you've earned it.

Thank you for reading *In Defense of the Grim Reaper*.
If you enjoyed a few laughs, please consider leaving
a review at your favorite retailer, and help others
discover books of spine-tingling humor.

Books in the In Defense Of series
In Defense of Babyhood
In Defense of Misfortune

Visit my author website
www.riyapresents.com

Made in the USA
Columbia, SC
27 October 2023

25087003R00033